No Lex 10·12

THE LIBRARY OF
AMERICAN
LIVES AND TIMES ™

BETSY ROSS

The American Flag
and Life in a Young America

Ryan P. Randolph

The Rosen Publishing Group's
PowerPlus Books ™
New York

*For the women in my life, especially Joanne, Lynda,
Margee, Phyllis, Becki, Ralane, and Raegan;
and in special memory of Virginia Botte*

Published in 2002 by The Rosen Publishing Group, Inc.
29 East 21st Street, New York, NY 10010

First Edition

*Editor's Note: All quotations have been reproduced as they appeared in
the letters and diaries from which they were borrowed. No correction was
made to the inconsistent spelling that was common in that time period.*

Library of Congress Cataloging-in-Publication Data

Randolph, Ryan P.
Betsy Ross : the American flag, and life in a young America / Ryan P.
Randolph.— 1st ed.
    p. cm. — (The library of American lives and times)
Includes bibliographical references and index.
  ISBN 0-8239-5730-6 (lib. bdg.)
1. Ross, Betsy, 1752–1836—Juvenile literature. 2. Revolutionaries—
United States—Biography—Juvenile literature. 3. United States—
History—Revolution, 1775–1783—Flags—Juvenile literature.
4. Philadelphia (Pa.)—Social life and customs—To 1775—Juvenile litera-
ture. [1. Ross, Betsy, 1752–1836. 2. Revolutionaries. 3. United States—
History—Revolution, 1775–1783. 4. Philadelphia (Pa.)—History—
Revolution, 1775–1783. 5. Flags. 6. Women—Biography.] I. Title.
II. Series.
  E302.6.R77 R36 2002
  973.3'092—dc21   2001000165

Manufactured in the United States of America

CONTENTS

1. The Life and Times of Betsy Ross, an Introduction

When we think of Betsy Ross, we think of her as the maker of the first American flag. The life of Betsy Ross was defined by much more than the American flag, though. Hers is the life of a pioneering woman and American patriot in a time when women were very limited in their options compared to men. Despite these limitations, Betsy Ross was a strong and courageous woman who did many things that were normally reserved for men, such as attending a formal school and running her own business. She faced many challenges in her life and accomplished many great things, even if we do not consider her role in the making of the first American flag.

Nonetheless, the American flag is a very important symbol to Americans, and Betsy Ross is best known as its creator. However, there is not much historical proof

Opposite: This is a detail of Betsy Ross from the painting entitled *The Birth of Our Nation's Flag* by Charles H. Weisgerber. Though there is not a lot of historical evidence behind it, Betsy Ross has long been considered the creator of the first American flag.

The American flag, to this day, symbolizes all that Americans
fought for during the Revolutionary War—liberty and democracy.
The only thing that has changed is the number of stars,
signifying the number of states that have joined the Union
since the original thirteen colonies declared independence in 1776.

to support this fact. Stories that Betsy Ross told to her
children and grandchildren, made public nearly one
hundred years after she would have sewn the first
flag, are some of the only evidence that points to her.
On the other hand, there is no evidence to disprove
her story or prove that anybody else made the first
American flag, either. Despite the lack of real historical evidence, Betsy Ross has become a symbol of
American ideals just the same, and she holds a very
special place in American history.

The creation of the first American flag was a very important contribution to history. Betsy Ross's association with this flag makes her an important figure in America's past and the events that have shaped the world we live in today. This is just one reason to take a closer look at Betsy Ross's life. Exploring Betsy Ross's life will help us to see what type of person she was. It may also help us determine whether it seems likely that the stories she told her children and grandchildren are accurate. Whatever one believes, her life story is an inspirational one of independence and courage that go beyond her association with the flag.

During her lifetime, Betsy Ross was shunned by her family and banished from the Quaker religion for marrying a man of a different religion. She lost two husbands in the fight for independence from Britain, and married three times. In a time when it was not very common for women to own businesses, Betsy Ross owned and operated an upholstery shop in Philadelphia. She was also the mother of seven children and lived to be eighty-four years old. Women in colonial times did not usually live that long. By learning about the trials and triumphs of Betsy Ross's life, we can learn about what it was like to live in colonial Philadelphia and how she earned such a unique place in American history.

2. Betsy Ross's Quaker Background

Betsy Ross's great-grandfather was named Andrew Griscom. He was a successful carpenter who emigrated from England to New Jersey. Griscom was a member of a religion called the Society of Friends, or Friends.

Since the 1700s, members of the Society of Friends have been more commonly known as Quakers. The Quaker religion is a Protestant religion, or a religion that broke away from, or protested against, the Catholic Church. Quakers have a very strong belief in Jesus and God, but they do not practice their beliefs in the same way as members of other Protestant religions. Quakers do not go to churches for services or Mass, but instead come together at simple meetinghouses for meetings. The meetings are not led by a priest or minister, and there are no sermons or sacraments. There are none of the things usually associated with church, such as music, singing, candles, or statues. During the meetings, Quakers pray directly to God and wait for God's Spirit to speak to them. This is called receiving the Inner Light. These practices are much the same today as they were in Betsy's time.

This is an undated engraving of the old Court House and Friends Meeting House, at the southwest corner of 2nd and Market Streets. The Meeting House, at the left in the picture, was originally built on ground donated by Quaker leader George Fox. The house was enlarged in 1755, then moved to Arch Street in 1808.

Why are Friends also called Quakers? This nickname for members of the Society of Friends goes back more than three hundred years. George Fox, one of the religion's founders, had to explain his radical and unorthodox religious views to a court in England. Fox told the court that even the judge must tremble and quake at the Word of the Lord. The judge then asked George Fox if he was a quaker. The Quaker nickname stuck and is now accepted by the Friends.

The Quakers were not very popular because of their unusual way of worshiping God. So, in 1681, William Penn purchased the land we know today as Pennsylvania for what was sometimes called a "Holy Experiment." The "Holy Experiment" was a colony

This engraved portrait of George Fox is based on a painting by S. Chinn. Fox lived from 1624 to 1691.

where the Quakers were free to practice their beliefs.

Pennsylvania is named after William Penn. He was the son of an English admiral to whom the king of England, Charles II, owed a large sum of money. Penn persuaded the king to charter a large tract of land west of New Jersey as a colony, instead of paying the money to the family. Penn was originally going to call the new colony Sylvania, but King Charles II suggested he call it Penn Sylvania, meaning Penn's Woods. The new colony became a place for Quakers to live without persecution and a center of religious freedom in the colonies.

Andrew Griscom decided to move from New Jersey to Philadelphia, Pennsylvania, a year after the colony was set up, to be part of the experiment. Griscom purchased 495 acres (200.3 ha) of land in the Spring Garden section, north of Philadelphia, and also received a plot of land within the city proper. He was soon married and had a family. Griscom set up his business in town and taught his son to be a carpenter. They both became well-respected carpenters in Philadelphia.

It seems that Andrew Griscom passed his skills on to his grandson, Samuel, as well. The names of Andrew

This is an undated wood engraving showing William Penn. In this scene, William Penn receives the charter of Pennsylvania from Charles II. He received the grant of land in New England as a payment of debt owed to his father.

Griscom's son and grandson can be seen inscribed on a wall in the Carpenters' Hall in Philadelphia. The Carpenters' Hall is the home of the oldest trade organization in the country, and it played host to both the first and second Continental Congresses which met before the Revolutionary War began.

Samuel Griscom, whose name appears in Carpenters' Hall, was Betsy Ross's father. He helped build the bell tower at the Pennsylvania State House, which is also known as Independence Hall. Without radios, television, or the Internet to provide news, bells like the one at the statehouse were very important.

Bells announced births and deaths, called people together to hear news and announcements, and signaled the open and close of markets.

Samuel Griscom married Rebecca James, who was also a follower of the Quaker religion. Rebecca was the daughter of a successful merchant from a wealthy Quaker family. Elizabeth Griscom, whom we know as Betsy Ross, was born in 1752 in West Jersey, Pennsylvania, outside of Philadelphia. Samuel and Rebecca Griscom had a big family—Betsy was the eighth of seventeen children that they had! During

This 1778 engraving, entitled *A N.W. View of the State House in Philadelphia taken 1778,* is by James Trenchard. It is based on a painting done by Charles Willson Peale. Samuel Griscom helped build the bell tower on the statehouse. The statehouse, now called Independence Hall, was the most ambitious public building in the colonies at the time. It took twenty-one years, from 1732 to 1753, to complete.

colonial times, families had many children and some of these children died young, but even by colonial standards the Griscom family was very large.

With the birth of Betsy and her brothers and sisters, the Griscom family was considered an established American family of four generations. In 1754, about two years after Betsy was born, the family moved into Philadelphia from West Jersey. Philadelphia was where Betsy's great-grandfather had settled, and it was where Samuel Griscom would build his own carpentry business successfully.

In the same year that Samuel Griscom moved back to Philadelphia, the relations between the Quakers and the people of other Protestant religions in Pennsylvania were going downhill. Besides being disliked for their unusual religious practices, the Quakers were criticized because they were against all fighting and war. In other words, they were pacifists. When William Penn received the land for his colony in 1681, he negotiated treaties with Native American tribes such as the Delaware and Shawnee, who already inhabited land in the area. Future generations of Quakers would honor these treaties despite criticism from other colonists.

The French and Indian War, which was being fought in 1754, tested the beliefs of the Quakers, many of whom held political offices and represented the Quaker people of the colony. The British, French, and Native American

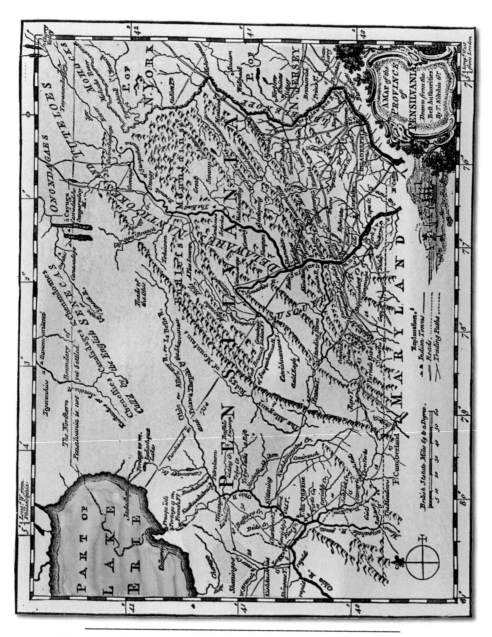

This map of Pennsylvania is a hand-colored woodcut made by T. Kitchin around 1756. This is how the colony would have looked when the Griscom family was establishing itself there in the early 1700s. Betsy spent her whole life living in this colony, which would become the site of so much activity in the Revolutionary War.

allies on each side had been struggling for control of North America and the rich natural resources and trade it had provided since 1645. Pennsylvania was one of the thirteen colonies that Britain was going to war to protect, and the Quakers were expected to help in this effort.

Despite pressure from other colonists and from the British government, the Quakers refused to fight in the war, especially against the Native American tribes with whom they had treaties. They resigned from the Pennsylvania Assembly in protest. Colonists with different beliefs quickly filled the vacated Quaker-held seats of the assembly. The French and Indian War further separated the Quaker community from the growing population of colonists in Pennsylvania and elsewhere who followed different religions.

3. Betsy Ross's Childhood

Growing up in the Quaker faith during colonial times probably made Betsy's childhood different from that of other children of her time, and very different from childhood today. Of course in colonial times, for any child, there were no computer games to play or cartoons to watch on television to pass the time away. For most children during colonial times, however, there were storybooks, card games, music, and dancing. Quaker children were not allowed to do any of these things. The Quaker religion was one of simplicity, and the people who followed it believed that living a simple life helped a person to avoid sin and prepare for life with God after death. This simple lifestyle also applied to Quaker children, and it prevented them from doing some of the things that other colonial children could do.

This did not mean that Betsy and other Quaker children could not have a fun childhood, however. With so many brothers and sisters, Betsy always had someone with whom she could play. Also, Quaker children could do some of the things that children today

This is an image of eighteenth-century girls jumping rope. Games such as this were common for children in colonial times, just as they are today. Quaker children were limited in the types of games they could play, but they were allowed to do some things that other children could not, such as attend formal schools—even the girls.

might do with their friends, such as swim, play tag or hide-and-seek in the summer, and sled and ice-skate in the winter.

When Betsy was not playing with friends or brothers and sisters, she did something that not many other girls did in colonial times. She went to a formal school. In a time when most girls were taught the basics of reading and writing at home, if they were taught at all, Betsy went to a Friends, or Quaker, public school, which taught both boys and girls.

School in colonial times was different than it is today. At the Friends public school, students were in class for eight hours a day, including Saturday. Teachers were usually very strict, and students were paddled or disciplined if they misbehaved or did not memorize their work. Students were taught the basics of reading, writing, and possibly some math.

Students at the Friends public school were also taught a basic skill or trade. Betsy liked to sew, and she spent much of her time learning this skill at school. She learned to sew clothes and quilts, among other items, such as samplers with the alphabet or prayers on them.

This is a typical sampler from colonial Philadelphia.
Sarah (Sally) Wister of Philadelphia, Pennsylvania, made
this sampler in 1773, using silk thread to embroider plain linen.

In 1764, Betsy finished her schooling. She was twelve years old. As a young woman, Betsy would learn to be a homemaker. This meant more than staying home and helping to look after the large Griscom family. It meant learning how to cook, clean, and probably manage the household money.

Around the same time that the Griscom family moved back into Philadelphia, ill feelings between the British government in London and the colonies in America were beginning to increase. There was a period of declining prosperity after the French and Indian War that was felt not only in the colonies but also by the British government. In the early 1760s, to make back some money spent on the war, Britain attempted to collect taxes, or duties, from the colonies. The colonists had always had a tax on many of the goods that came in and out of the busy port cities, but for the most part the taxes went unpaid. In fact, many merchants made a lot of money smuggling goods to avoid paying taxes.

The British parliament had not enforced the laws in the past because Britain still profited from the trade between itself and the colonies. During the French and Indian War, the ports of colonies were busy because they had to ship supplies to the British army, while

Following Spread (bottom half of page): This print shows the city and port of Old Philadelphia, with sailing ships entering the harbor. Note the elongated church steeples in the skyline. This was a common way for artists to indicate the piousness of a particular community.

also continuing to ship raw materials such as timber, tobacco, and cotton to Britain. This meant that there was more business and, therefore, more money in the colonies. Unfortunately, the French and Indian War cost Britain a lot of money. Britain was now looking for a way to make more money to pay off debts from the war. The end of the war also put an end to the large amounts of money that had been earned supplying the British war effort. This resulted in fewer jobs in the colonies, and, therefore, people had less money to buy the things they needed to live.

So, in 1760, after years of taxes that went uncollected and smuggling that deprived Britain of income,

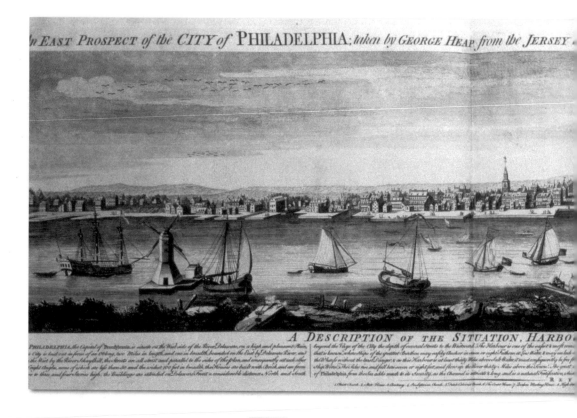

the British customs officials, or tax collectors, began to enforce the Navigation Acts, which the colonies had avoided for years. To enforce the collection of taxes, the tax collectors would search merchants' warehouses without permission, or forcefully seize and search the merchants' ships. The colonists chose not to argue about taxes, which might turn attention to the issue of smuggling. Instead, the colonists said that the merchants, as Englishmen, had a natural freedom from the illegal searches of property and seizure of goods used to collect taxes.

Increased taxes combined with a postwar depression in the economy meant that many colonists were

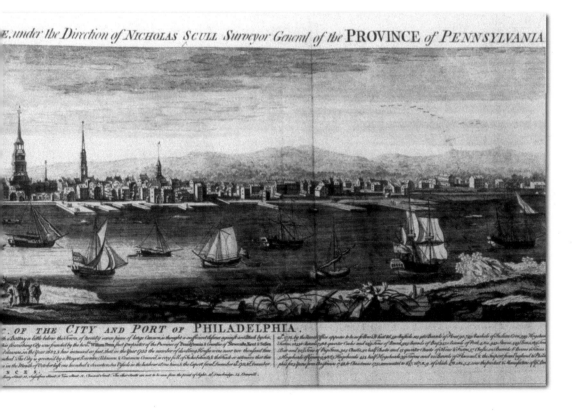

struggling to find work and facing bankruptcy. They started looking for someone to blame. They focused on King George III, Parliament, and the enforcement of taxes in the colonies. They claimed that Britain's enforcement of taxes, especially through search and seizure of property, was at the expense of their rights as Englishmen.

As tensions increased, almost every person in the colonies had to choose a side. The people in the colonies who continued to agree with the British were known as loyalists, or Tories. Often loyalists were important people, or they worked for the British as tax collectors or in other government positions. Those colonists who were against taxation without representation and who began talking of revolution were known as patriots, or Whigs.

The Quakers in Pennsylvania and other colonies were not necessarily loyalists, but many revolutionaries did not trust them because most Quakers would not openly support the patriot cause. In the late 1600s, King Charles II had personally granted the Quakers and William Penn a colony in which to practice their religion. Many colonists thought that the Quakers would want to keep close ties to England and the current king, George III, because of this. In reality, just like everywhere else in the colonies, the division of Quaker loyalties was split between patriots and loyalists.

Despite the rising tensions, Britain decided to collect a new tax from the colonies because the enforcement of old

This cartoon was published in a London paper on the day
King George III repealed the Stamp Act. The cartoon made
fun of First Lord of the Treasury George Grenville, here called
George Stamper, for this and other unpopular taxes he had passed.
Grenville carries a small coffin holding his "child," the Stamp Act.
The two banners represent the parliamentary votes against the act.

tax laws had not produced the money the British had expected. Britain still needed money to pay for the war, so Parliament passed the Stamp Act in 1765, very shortly after the Griscom family moved back into Philadelphia. The Stamp Act required that stamps be purchased to be attached to printed material, including many types of business documents and newspapers. Most of the colonies would not accept such an unfair tax from Britain, and there was so much protest about the Stamp Act that it was never enforced.

4. Betsy Ross's First Job and Marriage to John Ross

In 1764, the same year that Betsy finished school, Samuel Griscom moved his whole family to a house he had built on Arch Street in Philadelphia. His construction business had been quite successful since they had moved into the city. However, with tensions heating up between the colonists and the British, and the economy cooling down, it is likely that Samuel Griscom wanted to make sure his children would be able to support themselves if necessary. He took steps to make this possible.

Soon after the move, Betsy's father apprenticed her to a local upholsterer named John Webster. John Webster was a Quaker like the Griscoms, and his upholstery shop was well known in town for its high-quality work. In a trade like upholstery, an apprentice learned from a master and was given food and shelter in exchange for his or her work. After several years of learning, an apprentice could move on to start a business or get paid money for knowing a trade.

As a new apprentice, Betsy would not have done much actual sewing in the shop. She would have done basic chores such as running errands and keeping the shop clean while watching others do the sewing. In time, Betsy would begin to sew curtains and upholster chairs.

Betsy was not the only apprentice working at John Webster's upholstery shop. John Ross was an apprentice with Betsy, and they eventually became friends. John Ross was the son of an Episcopal, or Anglican, minister at Christ Church. Betsy and John Ross's friendship developed into love, and eventually, they wanted to get married. There was one major problem, though. Betsy was a Quaker and forbidden to marry outside of her religion.

The Quaker book, *The Rules of Discipline,* states: "Mixing in Marriage with

What is an upholsterer? Today we think of upholsterers as people who cover furniture with fabric, like sofa or chair makers. In colonial times upholsterers did many other sewing jobs as well. These jobs included making curtains, clothes, tablecloths, wallpaper made from fabric, umbrellas, and even flags. Betsy Ross's experience making flags may have helped her get the most important job of her life.

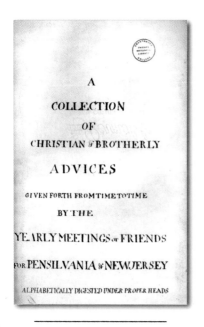

A

COLLECTION
OF
CHRISTIAN & BROTHERLY

ADVICES

GIVEN FORTH FROM TIME TO TIME

BY THE

YEARLY MEETINGS OF FRIENDS

FOR PENSILVANIA & NEW JERSEY

ALPHABETICALLY DIGESTED UNDER PROPER HEADS

This book, *The Rules of Discipline*, included various rules and advice for Christian behavior for the Quakers of Philadelphia and New Jersey.

those not of our Professions is an unequal Yoking which brings ill Consequences to the Parties as well as Grief to their honest Friends and Relatives and frequently ends in Woe and Ruin of Themselves and their Children." The penalty for marrying someone who was not a Quaker was harsh. Betsy would be "read out" of the Quaker meetinghouse. Being read out meant that Betsy would have to give up emotional and financial support from both her family and the Quaker community.

Despite all this, Betsy was a very strong and independent woman, and she would not be intimidated by her religion. She and John were both over twenty-one years old and could make their own decisions. They decided they loved each other so much that they would get married anyway. To support themselves, they would open their own upholstery shop so they could both work at the job they knew.

John Ross finished his apprenticeship with John Webster with enough knowledge to run an upholstery shop. He also had acquired a collection of the necessary

These upholstery tools are on display in Betsy Ross's workshop at the Betsy Ross House in Philadelphia. These are probably not the actual tools that she used, but they are typical upholstery tools from the time. From left to right, the tools are a copper oiler, a sewing box with thread, a betty lamp, a hammer, a tray holding tacks and nails, a needle, a file, an upholsterer's claw, a webber, and another claw.

tools from his training. He worked very hard to set up his own shop, and soon after he did, Betsy was also able to leave Webster's shop to work with John Ross.

Because of the conflict surrounding their marriage, Betsy and John Ross did not have a regular wedding. They eloped instead. On November 4, 1773, they were ferried across the Delaware River to Hugg's Tavern in New Jersey to be married. One of Betsy's sisters and her sister's husband took Betsy and John Ross across the river to New Jersey and witnessed the wedding. William Hugg, a family friend of Betsy's and owner of

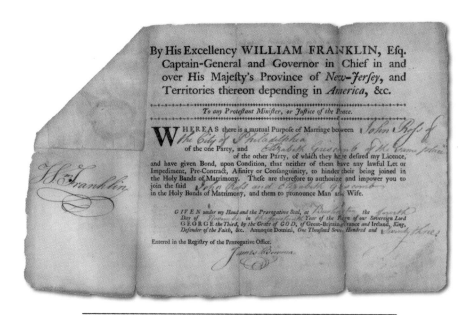

This is a copy of Betsy Ross and John Ross's
marriage license from New Jersey,
issued on November 4, 1773.

the tavern, was able to provide a place and a judge to
perform the marriage.

Soon after her marriage, Betsy Ross was read out of
the Quaker community and could no longer attend meetings. Her relationship with her parents was never the
same. They had never approved of John Ross, or Betsy's
marriage outside the faith. Both her parents and the
Quaker community tried to make her say that she had
made a mistake, but Betsy remained constant in her love
for John Ross and refused to change her mind.

Betsy Ross did not stop worshiping God after she
could no longer attend the Quaker meetings.

On Sundays, she began to attend Christ Church, where John Ross's father was a minister. John and Betsy Ross had their own pew at the church, and on some Sundays, they found George Washington sitting in the pew across from them.

Being read out by the Quakers hurt John and Betsy Ross's new business because they could not depend on the support of the large Quaker community in Philadelphia. Starting a new business is a lot of work anytime, and the city already had a number of upholstery shops. John and Betsy had a tough time getting loyal customers. They were struggling so much to make ends meet, they barely had time to leave the shop to get married.

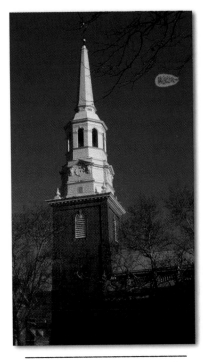

The Christ Church, built between 1722 and 1747, is a historic landmark of Philadelphia.

5. Philadelphia and the Coming Revolution

The upholstery business of Betsy and John Ross suffered for reasons other than their controversial marriage. Tensions between the British and the colonists had been growing for many years and now were reaching a boiling point. Betsy and John struggled to keep their business open, but they were not sure whether the trouble with the British would continue. This worried the couple. The actions of the British hurt their business because it had become harder to get supplies. Not only that, but because everyone had less money, fewer people could afford the upholstery services that John and Betsy offered.

Shortly after their marriage in late 1773, an express rider from Boston came to town announcing the events of the Boston Tea Party, which had occurred a few days earlier. The express rider was Paul Revere, and he came with news that colonists in Boston had staged a protest against a new tax imposed by the British, the Tea Act. A group of men called the Sons of Liberty had dressed up as Mohawk Indians and had thrown the British tea shipment into Boston Harbor.

Boston was not the only place where there were protests against the tax on tea. In Philadelphia, a ship that arrived with British tea turned around and left when the captain heard about the large crowd that had gathered in protest. The crowd also threatened the two Quaker business-men who had organized the shipment of tea to Philadelphia. One of the Quaker businessmen was related to Betsy Ross, but Betsy and John Ross sup-ported the colonists who were against the British, as did many other Quaker men and women.

This is the Betsy Ross House and upholstery shop on Arch Street. Betsy never owned this house, built in 1740, but rented it from 1773 to 1786. Before 1773, the Rosses lived next door, but Betsy would later move in and open her shop here.

The Boston Tea Party outraged the king, and Parliament soon passed the Coercive Acts. These acts were known as the Intolerable Acts to the colonists. The Acts were "intolerable" because they closed the port of Boston, restricted town meetings, and canceled the Massachusetts colonial charter, basically revoking the Massachusetts colonists' right to govern themselves.

Why did Boston colonists throw tea into the harbor, anyway? They did this in response to the Tea Act, passed by the British parliament. To help the British East India Company raise money for expansion in India, Parliament imposed a tax on tea in both England and the colonies. To the colonists, the Tea Act was another example of the British imposing their power with total disregard for the colonists' rights. The price of tea was set artificially low, and only certain merchants were allowed to sell the cheap tea. Many of the colonies were very angry and resisted the tax. Despite this, the British government still ordered the tea to be sent to the colonies. On November 27, 1773, the Dartmouth, Eleanor, *and* Beaver, *three ships loaded with tea from the East India Company, landed at Boston but were prevented from unloading their cargo. Threatening retribution if the tea was not returned to where it came from, the Sons of Liberty, led by Samuel Adams, met to determine the fate of the three cargo ships in Boston Harbor. On December 16, 1773, the fateful Boston Tea Party occurred.*

This undated lithograph shows the Boston Tea Party of December 16, 1773. The men in the boat were patriots dressed as Mohawk Indians. In protest against a tax on tea, they threw the contents of 342 chests of tea into Boston Harbor, while Boston residents cheered them on. The British punished the colonists with the Coercive, or Intolerable, Acts.

When news of the Intolerable Acts reached the colonies, leaders in Boston developed the Suffolk Resolves in response. The Suffolk Resolves declared the actions of the British unlawful and urged resistance against them. The British did not really expect the colonies, which were all very different and far apart, to be able to work together and support each other.

Unfortunately for Britain, the colonies were able to work together quite effectively. Towns had begun to organize Committees of Correspondence to keep one another informed of the events in their areas.

In September 1774, representatives from each colony arrived in Philadelphia for the First Continental Congress. The only colony that was not represented was Georgia, which could not attend the event. The colonial leaders in Georgia sent word that they would approve and support any plans made at the meeting. On the first day of the event, Patrick Henry of Virginia called on the representatives to think of themselves as Americans, not as people from their individual colonies. It would be the only way they could win a war against Britain.

6. The Revolutionary War Begins

Over the next several weeks, the Continental Congress adopted many of the Suffolk Resolves. The most important resolve stated that the colonies would muster troops and organize a defense against the British army. Many towns already had militias, or groups of citizen soldiers, who protected the towns in times of danger. Some of these militias had experience fighting beside the British army during the French and Indian War. This time, though, their skills would be used to fight against British rule rather than to protect it.

When the First Continental Congress finished meeting in October 1774, they made a plan to meet again in May 1775. Before they got that chance, news arrived in Philadelphia that the Battle of Lexington and Concord had been fought on April 19, 1775. The first fighting between the colonists and the British army had broken out, and the Revolutionary War had begun.

On May 10, 1775, the Continental Congress met in Philadelphia for the second time. The Second Continental Congress decided in favor of revolution and the formation

This is a hand-colored engraving by Amos Doolittle, based on eyewitness reports of the battles at Lexington and Concord. There are six labels in the image explaining the positions of the British and colonial troops, who fired first, and various other details about the battle scene at Lexington. Doolittle made four panels describing different parts of the battles that occurred around Lexington and Concord that day.

of an army. George Washington was named the commander of the new Continental army. On June 23, 1775, Washington and his new army marched from Philadelphia toward Boston to meet the British army.

Throughout the colonies, men were joining the army or their local militias to fight for American independence. John Ross joined the Philadelphia militia, called the Citizen's Guard. Like other fellow patriots, John Ross was willing to stand up to the British if necessary. Before the Revolution reached Philadelphia, much of

This is a 1760 portrait of George Washington by James Peale. Washington was commander of the Continental army during the war and the first president once independence was won.

the job of the Citizen's Guard was training, stockpiling, and guarding military supplies and ammunition stored in the city. One night, while John Ross was guarding the supplies, the ammunition caught fire and exploded. John was badly injured, and some fellow patriots brought him home to Betsy. She tried to nurse him back to health, but the burial book at Christ Church indicates that he died on January 21, 1776.

Betsy Ross was now a widow and had some difficult decisions to make in challenging times. She decided to keep the upholstery business that she and John had worked so hard on and run it herself. In colonial times, it was not common for women to own and run businesses, but often a widow was allowed to take on the business of her husband when he passed away. Betsy Ross was a strong and independent woman, and like some widowed colonial women, she kept the business and ran it herself. She could have gone back to her family, or possibly back to John Webster's upholstery shop. Instead, Betsy Ross decided to make it on her own.

Shortly before John Ross passed away in late January 1776, Washington's army had arrived in Boston. They met the local members of the Massachusetts militia and engaged in a siege of the city of Boston, which was occupied by the British at the time. Washington decided that, to demonstrate the American willingness to fight for their independence and to encourage patriotism in his troops, he needed to fly a flag as a symbol.

The flag chosen was called the Grand Union. It had horizontal stripes similar to the ones on the current

This is a reproduction of a colonial Grand Union flag. Washington used it to rally his troops during their siege of Boston. However, because it used the British flag in the corner, the British thought it meant Washington wanted to surrender. Washington quickly realized he needed a new flag.

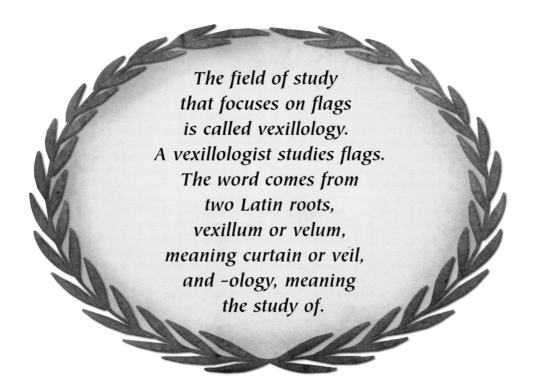

*The field of study
that focuses on flags
is called vexillology.
A vexillologist studies flags.
The word comes from
two Latin roots,
vexillum or velum,
meaning curtain or veil,
and -ology, meaning
the study of.*

American flag, and a symbol that looked like the British flag, or a Union Jack, in the upper left corner. This Union Jack symbol is actually the red cross of St. George, the symbol for England, and the white cross of St. Andrew, a symbol of Scotland.

The Grand Union design may have been chosen because the colonists still considered themselves part of Britain at the beginning of the Revolution. The British occupying Boston and their loyalist supporters thought that this flag meant Washington was going to surrender. This was not what Washington and the Americans were doing at all. It was time for a new flag.

7. The Story of the First American Flag

In March 1776, the British decided to abandon Boston. They were going to concentrate their army on attacking the colonies from Canada, and possibly New York. After the British withdrew, fighting resumed and the Revolutionary War continued throughout the spring of 1776. The American army did not do well against the British coming down from Canada. George Washington and the Revolutionary leaders decided to return to Philadelphia to regroup and prepare for a possible attack by the British from New York.

This is important because some historians think that George Washington was not in Philadelphia when Betsy Ross was said to have met him. In late May or early June 1776, a few months after the death of her husband, Betsy Ross said that she had a meeting with George Washington, George Ross, and Robert Morris in

Right: This map shows the colonies at the beginning of the Revolution. In the early part of the war, much of the fighting occurred in the Northeast, and Canada. Soon the British were threatening New York and the colonies further south. Philadelphia was a good central location from which Washington could coordinate military operations.

THE UNITED COLONIES

AT THE

her upholstery shop. The three men were part of a committee in charge of creating and getting Congress's approval for a flag for the new country. This is only according to Betsy Ross's stories to her children, because the journals of the Continental Congress do not mention a small committee formed to work on a flag.

Nevertheless, it is said that these three men chose to visit the house and upholstery shop of Betsy Ross to seek her help in making the first American flag.

The three men who came to her house were important men in Congress and leaders of the Revolution. George Washington was the leader of the Continental army at the time. He may have known Betsy Ross

This engraving of the influential Robert Morris was based on a drawing by Alonzo Chappel.

from the Christ Church, which they both attended. Washington was also said to have hired Betsy Ross to sew his shirts. He may have remembered Betsy Ross as a capable upholsterer able to meet the task of sewing a flag. Robert Morris was also an important patriot and politician from Pennsylvania. Morris was known as the financier of the Revolution because he gave

This engraving of George Ross was made by an unknown artist around 1770.

a lot of money to General George Washington and the army, and also helped raise money from other wealthy patriots.

George Ross is believed to have been an uncle of John Ross, Betsy Ross's husband. He was a lawyer and a popular member of the Continental Congress from Pennsylvania. Illness cut short George Ross's political career, and he died just three years after he signed the Declaration of Independence. Some people believe that George Ross may have known Betsy and her skills as an upholsterer because of his relation to John Ross.

Betsy Ross's daughter, Rachel Fletcher, recalled of the committee that "I remember to have heard her also say that it was made on the order of a

In 1925, a safe belonging to a descendant of Samuel Wetherhill was found and opened. Samuel Wetherhill was a close friend of Betsy Ross and a member of the Free Quakers, as she was. In the safe was a folded, five-pointed paper star, possibly the very one Betsy Ross showed to Washington. The paper star was signed by Betsy Ross's daughter Clarissa. Some people say that Samuel Wetherill and his family would not have saved the paper star unless they realized how important it could be.

Committee, of whom Colonel Ross was one, and that Robert Morris was also one of the Committee. That General Washington, acting in conference with the Committee, called with them at her house." The house referred to was Betsy's new home and upholstery shop, located on Arch Street next door to the house she lived in with John Ross.

Betsy's daughter recalls Betsy saying that she "was previously well acquainted with Washington, and that he had often been in her house in friendly visits, as well as on business. That she had embroidered ruffles for his shirt bosoms and cuffs, and that it was partly owing to his

This is the Continental navy flag with a picture of a rattlesnake saying, "Don't tread on me." This was a warning to the British that the colonies would fight back. It also symbolized that the American colonists were like a rattlesnake—they would strike only if they were in danger or provoked. The thirteen pieces of the rattle meant that the thirteen colonies' protests would be heard only if they were united.

friendship for her that she was chosen to make the flag." It is interesting to note that George Washington wrote many letters and diaries of his actions, but his visit to Betsy Ross with the committee was recorded only by Betsy and her family, not by Washington.

Betsy Ross often told her children that when the three distinguished men came to the upholstery shop with their design, she suggested some changes. The design for the flag probably came from the old Grand Union flag, combined with some of the newer designs being used in the colonies and the individual units, or regiments, in the army and navy. With the large number of colorful and different flags around, the new American flag would have to be one in which everyone could take pride.

According to Rachel Fletcher, "She said it was square and a flag should be one third longer than its width, that the stars were scattered promiscuously over the field, and she said they should be either in lines or in some adopted form as a circle, or a star." More important for the flag that Americans use today, Betsy Ross suggested that the six-pointed stars of the original design be dropped in favor of five-pointed stars.

A niece of Betsy Ross also recalled Betsy saying that she recommended a change to the star on the original

---

Next Spread: This 1930 oil painting, entitled *Betsy Ross & The First Stars & Stripes—1777,* is by James Ward Dunmore. It shows the meeting between Betsy Ross and the Flag Committee—George Washington, George Ross, and Robert Morris. Betsy Ross and two girls, probably her daughters, are showing the designed flag to the men.

design. She said Betsy Ross then "showed them how to fold a piece of paper in the proper manner, and with one cut of the scissors, to make a five-pointed star."

Betsy Ross was probably hesitant to present her ideas to such important leaders, but once she did they were taken into account. Washington was said to be the most active of the three in the flag committee that went to see Betsy Ross. According to the recollection passed on to her children and grandchildren, Washington made some modifications to the original design based on Betsy's recommendations. This modified design seems to be the one the committee requested that she make.

Betsy Ross's flag had the same seven red stripes and six white stripes that are on the flag today. In the left-hand corner of the flag, or the canton, she sewed a series of thirteen white, five-pointed stars on a blue background. According to Betsy Ross's story, she worked on the flag soon after she received the final design. She handed back her finished work to the congressional committee in the same month they had come to see her. She was not sure if her flag would be the one chosen. In the end, it was the design that would become the first flag of America.

8. The Revolutionary War Comes Close to Home

Thus far, the American army had been doing poorly against the British forces attacking from Canada, in what is today upstate New York. The Continental army lost New York City to the British and, in the later part of 1776, began to retreat into New Jersey, toward Philadelphia. Soon after Washington was said to have met with Betsy Ross, he was off to meet the British, who were advancing from New York. Philadelphia is relatively close to New York and would have been easy to get to through New Jersey, or by water along the East Coast and up the Delaware River.

By the beginning of December 1776, a call had gone out urging all patriots, ages sixteen to sixty, to fight against the British. On December 26, 1776, George Washington was able to salvage an inspiring victory from a rough year of losses. He and his men crossed the Delaware River during a snowstorm and attacked the British at Trenton, New Jersey. At last, they met with success. Most of the enemy soldiers captured were Hessians, or German mercenaries, who were then

This 1851 painting entitled *Washington Crossing the Delaware* is by Emanuel Gottlieb Leutze. This painting showing Washington's heroic December 26 crossing is more romantic than historical. The crossing actually happened in the middle of the night, but the artist uses the symbolism of Washington leading his men out of the darkness into a new dawn. Leutze also shows the "Betsy Ross flag" flying overhead, but it was not designed until six months after the battle.

marched through Philadelphia to show the public the Continental army's victory over the British.

Washington followed up the victory over the British in Trenton with a similar attack and victory in Princeton, New Jersey. The British were forced back to New York for the rest of the winter, while George Washington and his men spent the winter in Morristown, New Jersey. In many wars of the time, troops did not fight as much in the winter because of the harsh weather conditions.

With the defeats in Princeton and Trenton, the British no longer threatened to invade Philadelphia.

What is a Hessian?
A Hessian is a German
mercenary, or soldier-for-hire,
used by the British army during
the American Revolution.
Because Germany was not yet
a country, these soldiers were known
by the state that they came from,
named Hesse. Hesse became
part of Germany
in 1871.

For many shopkeepers like Betsy Ross, this was a relief, as the businesses could be reopened. It was still very hard to get the necessary supplies to run the upholstery business, and the number of people who needed upholstery services during the war was small. Nonetheless, it seems that Betsy Ross did a good amount of business making flags for different military groups during the Revolutionary War.

During the early spring of 1777, there is evidence that Betsy Ross was doing some upholstery work for the Pennsylvania navy. The minutes of the State Navy Board of Pennsylvania for May 29, 1777, say in part,

Die Hessen, vom General Washington am 25ten Dec: 1776. zu Trenton überfallen, werden als Kriegsgefangne in Philadelphia eingebracht.

This undated engraving by German artist Daniel N. Chodowiecki shows the Hessian soldiers captured in the Battle of Trenton. They are being taken to Philadelphia by General George Washington and his troops. The caption on the engraving says this parade occurred on December 25, 1776, but it actually happened on the day after Christmas.

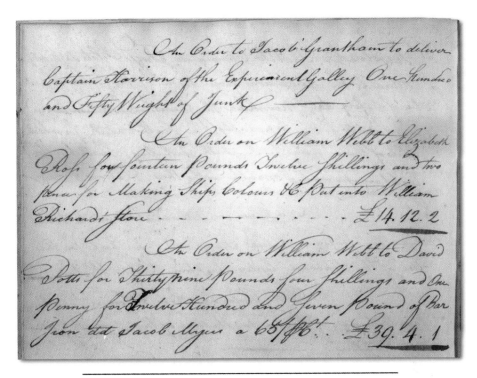

These are the minutes from the State Navy Board of Pennsylvania stating that Betsy Ross had been commissioned to make the flags for their ships. Her name is highlighted in pink here. Because her services were requested by one government agency, it seems more likely that she could have been chosen by George Washington and his flag committee as well.

"An order on William Webb to Elizabeth Ross for fourteen pounds, twelve shillings, and two pence, for making ship's colours, &c, put into Richards store." Betsy Ross's work for the Navy proves that Betsy Ross did make flags. Also, because she was making flags for the state government, it is not as difficult to believe that she might have been chosen to make the first flag for the Continental Congress.

On June 14, 1777, the Second Continental Congress passed a resolution concerning the flag of the new

United States. This was about one year after Betsy Ross was said to have been visited by George Washington, Robert Morris, and George Ross. The resolution read, "Resolved that the Flag of the united states be 13 stripes alternate red and white, that the Union be 13 stars white in a blue field representing a new constellation."

This resolution probably made Betsy Ross very proud and happy. She would have been happy to contribute to the war effort, not to mention happy to get the business that would result from requests for the new flag. Betsy Ross was not the only one to see increased business resulting from orders for new

Above is a manuscript of the resolution passed by the Second Continental Congress about the flag. The resolution, highlighted in blue, was passed on June 14, 1777. Today June 14 is the national holiday, Flag Day.

This is a variation on the thirteen-star U.S. flag from colonial times. Because the only rules for the flag were that the stripes alternate between red and white and that there be stars in a blue field, many different variations were created. The stars in this flag have six points rather than the five recommended by Betsy Ross, and they are arranged in a semicircle. Eventually the flag would become standardized.

American flags. Many other flag makers around the colonies would receive orders for them as well.

These flag makers did not necessarily follow the design that Betsy Ross created. The loose specifications given in the resolution meant that different people could interpret the new flag design in different ways. It did not say how many points the stars should have, and stars on flags varied from five to eight points. There was also no specification on how the stars should be arranged. People made flags that had stars in circles,

Henry Mosler made this 1911 picture of Betsy Ross and some girls sewing the new American flag. The room that the women are sitting in is the same one in which Betsy met with the flag committee. After the resolution for the flag was passed on June 14, 1777, there probably was an increase in flag orders for Betsy and other upholsterers.

squares, lines, and other positions. Finally, there was no specification on which way the thirteen stripes were to alternate, so there could be seven white stripes and six red stripes instead of the other way around—seven red stripes and six white stripes as they appear on the flag today.

On June 15, 1777, the day after the flag resolution was passed in the Second Continental Congress, Betsy Ross married again. Betsy Ross had been a widow for about a year and a half before marrying merchant

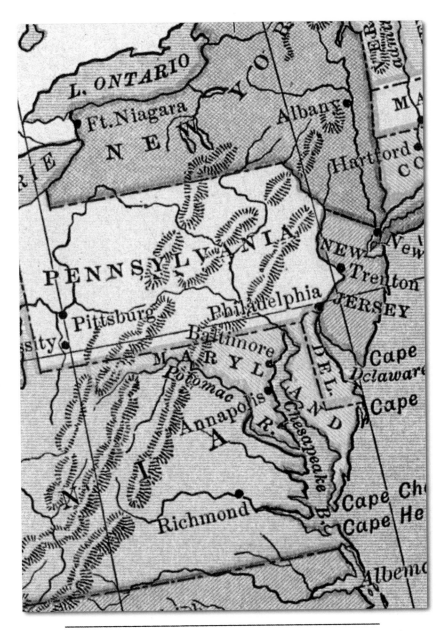

By early 1777, the British were in New Jersey and guarding the American coastlines. This made sailing down Chesapeake Bay and out of Philadelphia a dangerous undertaking for the colonists. British ship captains knew that stopping merchant vessels from trading and bringing supplies back to the colonies would put pressure on the colonists to give up their fight for independence.

57

sea-captain Joseph Ashburn. She became Betsy Ross Ashburn. The new couple had been introduced through one of Betsy Ross's brothers-in-law who had worked with Joseph Ashburn.

In late 1776 and early 1777, the British were in New Jersey and guarding the waters off the coast of America, so sailing from Philadelphia was dangerous for the colonists. Even without a blockade by the British navy, sailing in the wintertime, with cold weather and frequent storms, was difficult. Joseph Ashburn spent the winter in Philadelphia, where he visited Betsy Ross before the wedding. They decided that after the marriage Betsy would keep running her shop, and when conditions permitted, Joseph would sail out on his ship, the *Swallow*.

During the war, Joseph Ashburn became a privateer. This meant that he was allowed to attack and board British ships. Whatever he found, he and his crew could keep. Shortly after Betsy Ross married Joseph Ashburn, he was able to sail the *Swallow* past the British blockade and toward the West Indies in the Caribbean Sea.

9. The British in Philadelphia

In the summer of 1777, the British again attacked from New York. General Washington received word that the British army was landing a large number of soldiers in New Jersey, just 60 miles (96.6 km) from Philadelphia. On August 24, the Continental army marched through Philadelphia to meet the British army. Some people of the time noted how unprepared the new Continental army looked, without uniforms, weapons, or enough supplies.

Joseph Ashburn also arrived back from his trip to the West Indies in August 1777. Betsy and Joseph were happy to be together, but Joseph was gone again very soon. He and the crew of the *Swallow* were working with the Navy to help guard the forts held by the Americans on the Delaware River near Philadelphia. Besides protecting the forts, the *Swallow* probably was used to ship supplies to the different forts as well.

The British army finally met the Americans at the Battle of Brandywine Creek on September 11, 1777. It had been a few weeks since the British had landed in New Jersey, and since Washington and the American

The Battle of Brandywine Creek occurred on September 11, 1777, near Chadds Ford, Pennsylvania. The British forces, in red above, numbered about 18,000, and the Americans, dressed in blue, had 11,000 men. Nine hundred Americans were killed or wounded, and 400 were taken prisoner. The British casualties totaled 600 men.

troops had marched through Philadelphia. The battle took place just 25 miles (40.2 km) from Philadelphia, and the British forced the Continental army back toward the city. The battlefront was moving steadily toward the city of Philadelphia.

The defeat of the American troops so close to the city threw Philadelphia into chaos. The men of the Continental Congress fled the city to Lancaster, Pennsylvania. Many patriots piled wagons full of their belongings and fled town as well. Some people even buried their silver and other valuables so that the invading British army could not get them. Many of the loyalists who had fled the city earlier in the war began to come back into Philadelphia in advance of the British.

Joseph Ashburn was one of the patriots who fled the city. He quickly set out to sea on the *Swallow*. As a privateer, he would have been in danger if he had stayed. Many businesspeople shut down their shops and fled the city, but not Betsy Ross. She stayed to protect her house and her business as best she could. The only people who stayed in Philadelphia in the face of the invading British were women, children, those who could not afford to leave, loyalists who were supporting the British, and many of the pacifist Quakers.

On September 26, 1777, the British entered Philadelphia. The British soldiers were better equipped than the American troops that had marched through the city a little more than a month earlier, but they were still lacking in supplies and food.

Not only did the British army invade the city, but the troops stayed in the houses of many people around the city. The soldiers had to sleep somewhere during the winter ahead, so this seemed the best solution. Even Betsy Ross may have had to take a few British soldiers into her house. The British soldiers probably first took over the many empty houses of the people who had already left the city, but there were still many people remaining who had to accept the soldiers into their homes.

Howard Pyle painted this scene of the 1777 attack upon Cliveden, or the Benjamin Chew House, in 1898. The attack occurred during the Battle of Germantown in October 1777. British troops had taken over the large home and were using it as a fort. American soldiers stormed the house, but the British were well protected behind the stone walls. The Americans suffered a bloody defeat.

Winter was coming upon the city of Philadelphia, and the conditions were very poor, especially for the citizens who did not leave the city. The British troops were hungry and cold, and they took what they needed from the citizens of Philadelphia. Jewelry and valuable objects were taken from homes, and the troops ate all of the food they could find. With the onset of a cold winter, furniture and other wooden objects were used in fires to warm the soldiers, and the citizens had to resort to burning household objects to stay warm. The churches and other large buildings were used as hospitals to treat the British soldiers wounded in the battles going on around the city. This was a very frightening time for Betsy Ross.

The war continued to rage outside of Philadelphia, as George Washington and the Continental army fought to end the British occupation of the important city. In October 1777, the Continental army was again defeated by the British in the long and sometimes confusing Battle of Germantown in Pennsylvania. Many British and American soldiers were killed.

After the win at Germantown, the British army and navy began to press the American strategic positions at forts along the Delaware River. In November 1777, the

This is an undated painting of George Washington at the Battle of Germantown by Alonzo Chappell. This was a bloody battle for both sides, shown here by the dead and wounded British and Continental men scattered throughout the scene.

British were finally able to defeat the Americans and take over Fort Mifflin. General George Washington and the Continental army retreated to Valley Forge, Pennsylvania, for the long winter of 1777–1778.

The British army in Philadelphia decided not to attack the American troops at Valley Forge, but instead tried to search out American merchants and patriots along the shores and waterways around Philadelphia and New Jersey. The British wanted to focus their

This 1777 map of the plan of the attack on Fort Mifflin is attributed to Simon Fraser. It comes from the collection of General Sir Henry Clinton, commander of British troops during the Revolution. It defines the position of the British batteries, the number of guns present, and the channel used to reach the more vulnerable side of Fort Mifflin. *Somerset* is shown, as are other ships positioned in waterways around the fort.

efforts on stopping the privateers who had been attacking British ships. These privateers currently were hiding in these waterways, often in small groups. It was easier to look for groups of privateer ships during the winter months than to attack what remained of the Continental army at Valley Forge.

Despite avoiding British attacks, the winter at Valley Forge was not easy for the Continental army. They had to survive a very hard winter, in snow and bitter cold. There was very little food and not enough shoes or warm clothes for the soldiers. Though some patriotic soldiers were able to last the hard winter, many men deserted the Continental army, or died of cold, starvation, and sickness. The regular British soldiers were better off in Philadelphia, but only a little bit. They were hungry and cold while the more important officers in the Army were always warm, well fed, and even entertained by plays and dances.

In the spring of 1778, news reached the British that their old enemy, France, had decided to support the Americans. The British officers in Philadelphia felt that they risked being trapped in the city by the French who could blockade the Delaware River. The British also thought that the French might try to attack New York, so they wanted to concentrate some of their forces there. Around May or June 1778, the British and their loyalist supporters quickly boarded ships and barges and sailed for New York.

This engraving shows George Washington meeting with Marquis de Lafayette at Valley Forge. The winter at Valley Forge was a harsh one for the American troops. Men were starving and freezing to death. Many soldiers chose to desert the army during this winter. Washington was proud of the men who chose to remain and who put the American cause above the hard sacrifices they were making.

Almost as quickly as the British had taken over Philadelphia, they left the city. There were a lot of celebrations as American soldiers were released from prison and many patriots returned to the city. In the summer of 1778, Betsy Ross was finally reunited with her husband Joseph Ashburn after many months of separation.

The reunion was temporary because, as soon as it was possible, Joseph Ashburn went to sea again and slipped past the British blockade down to the West Indies. As a

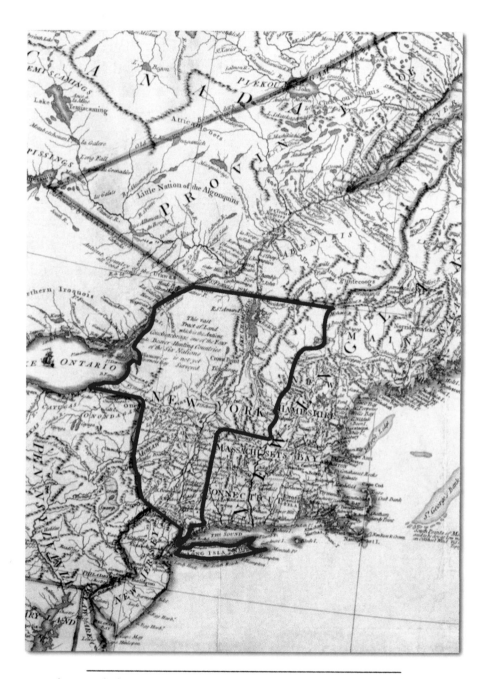

This English map, *The Seat of War in the Northern Colonies*, was printed in London a little over a month after the Declaration of Independence was signed in Philadelphia. It shows Quebec, New England, New York, and New Jersey. Purple depicts New York, where the British went when they pulled out of Philadelphia.

privateer with his own ship, Joseph helped his country and provided for his wife. He would also need to provide for a new child because in September 1779, Betsy Ross and Joseph Ashburn had their first child, Zillah. Joseph was able to make the trip between Philadelphia and the West Indies successfully several times.

While the Revolutionary War moved to the southern colonies, Joseph continued to make trips to the West Indies for supplies. In October 1780, he left on his final trip. Betsy Ross would never see him again. Betsy was pregnant with their second child, but Joseph would never meet her. The second daughter of Betsy and Joseph, named Eliza, was born in February 1781.

10. The End of the Revolutionary War

In 1781, the Revolutionary War was turning around for the Americans. In March 1781, the Articles of Confederation, the first governing document of the United States, was passed into law. Betsy Ross was still running her upholstery business but also searching for clues as to the location of her lost husband, Joseph Ashburn. She did not know if he had died, in the fighting or in a shipwreck, or if he was still alive.

By October 1781, the British surrendered to the Americans at Yorktown. Though a treaty officially ending the war would not be signed until 1783, the Revolutionary War was over. Unfortunately, Betsy Ross still did not know what had happened to her husband. When an old friend of hers, John Claypoole, arrived home, he told of his imprisonment in Old Mill with Joseph Ashburn. Old Mill was a prison in England where many patriot sailors captured in the war were sent. It was known as a prison where inmates were treated harshly. John Claypoole informed Betsy Ross that Joseph had passed away from illness as a prisoner of the British.

ARTICLES

OF

CONFEDERATION AND PERPETUAL UNION,

BETWEEN THE COLONIES OF

NEW-HAMPSHIRE,
MASSACHUSETTS-BAY,
RHODE-ISLAND,
CONNECTICUT,
NEW-YORK,
NEW-JERSEY,
PENNSYLVANIA,

THE COUNTIES OF NEW-CASTLE,
KENT AND SUSSEX ON DELAWARE,
MARYLAND,
VIRGINIA,
NORTH-CAROLINA,
SOUTH-CAROLINA, AND
GEORGIA.

ART. I. THE Name of this Confederacy shall be "THE UNITED STATES OF AMERICA."

ART. II. The said Colonies unite themselves so as never to be divided by any Act whatever, and hereby severally enter into a firm League of Friendship with each other, for their common Defence, the Security of their Liberties, and their mutual and general Welfare, binding the said Colonies to assist one another against all Force offered to or attacks made upon them or any of them, on Account of Religion, Sovereignty, Trade, or any other Pretence whatever.

ART. III. Each Colony shall retain and enjoy as much of its present Laws, Rights and Customs, as it may think fit, and reserves to itself the sole and exclusive Regulation and Government of its internal police, in all matters that shall not interfere with the Articles of this Confederation.

ART. IV. No Colony or Colonies, without the Consent of the United States assembled, shall send any Embassy to or receive any Embassy from, or enter into any Treaty, Convention or Conference with the King or Kingdom of Great-Britain, or any foreign Prince or State, nor shall any Colony or Colonies, nor any Person or Persons of the United States, or of any Colony or Colonies, accept of any Present, Emolument, Office, or Title of any Kind whatever, from the King or Kingdom of Great-Britain, or any foreign Prince or State; nor shall the United States assembled, or any Colony grant any Title of Nobility.

ART. V. No two or more Colonies shall enter into any Treaty, Confederation or Alliance whatever between them, without the previous and free Consent and Allowance.

The Articles of Confederation were agreed to by Congress on November 15, 1777. Over the next several years, the articles were sent to the states for ratification. After Maryland ratified the document on March 1, 1781, the Articles of Confederation were officially put into effect.

This drawing of Old Mill prison in Plymouth, England, was created between 1840 and 1850. Betsy's second husband, Joseph Ashburn, would die while imprisoned here. Harsh treatment and poor conditions would cause many prisoners to fall ill and die at Old Mill.

After the death of Joseph Ashburn, John and Betsy renewed their friendship and began to spend more time together. Both Betsy Ross and John Claypoole had been brought up in the Quaker religion around Philadelphia. They had known each other as children, and Betsy probably kept in touch with John's sisters as well. The friendship between John Claypoole and Betsy Ross soon blossomed into a romance. In May 1783, Betsy Ross was married to John Claypoole, becoming Betsy Ross Ashburn Claypoole.

During this time, the British and Americans were negotiating a peace treaty. Life for Betsy and John Claypoole was already settling down. Betsy had convinced John to give up his life as a sailor, and, for a while, John worked with Betsy in the upholstery shop. John probably brought some experience and new business to the shop. The new couple settled down in Philadelphia and had a large family. Betsy had five daughters by John, named Clarissa Sidney, Susannah, Rachel, Jane, and Harriet. Sadly, Harriet died a few months after birth.

John and Betsy were raised as Quakers, but both had started attending Christ Church in Philadelphia, which is where they were married. Betsy had married someone outside of the Quaker religion and had supported the war effort when she could. John Claypoole had been an active soldier in the Revolutionary War, and it is probable that he spent the winter with the Continental army at Valley Forge. All these things were against the Society of Friends' beliefs. Participating in the war was particularly bad and went against the Quakers' belief in pacifism and their instructions for members not to fight against the British.

In 1783, Betsy Ross and John Claypoole stopped attending Christ Church and joined the Society of Free Quakers. The Society of Free Quakers was also called the Fighting Quakers. These were people brought up in the Quaker religion, but who went

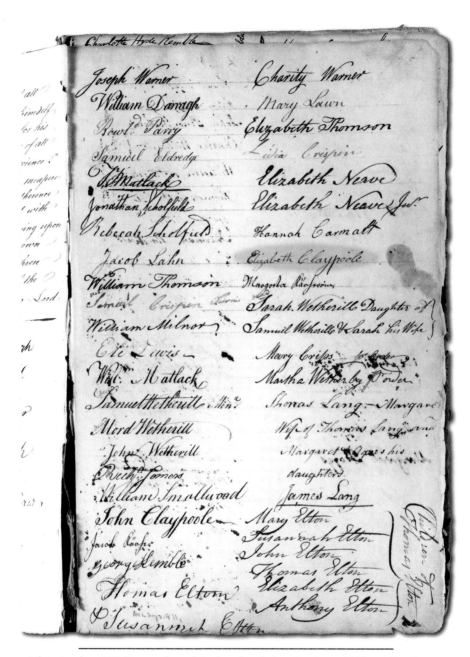

This is the 1785 membership book of the Society of Free Quakers. All members of the society signed their names in this book. Betsy Ross's name, signed Elizabeth Claypoole, is highlighted in green.

The Free Quakers had been meeting since about 1781, but they opened their own meetinghouse in 1783. It still stands as a monument in Philadelphia on the southwest corner of 5th and Arch Streets. The meetinghouse is not open often, but there is an interesting dedication on the outside of the building: "By General Subscription for the FREE QUAKERS Erected in the YEAR of OUR LORD 1783 of the EMPIRE 8." Nobody really knows what the Empire 8 means. Perhaps these patriots believed that the new United States would become a great empire. Betsy Ross and John Price Wetherill eventually decided to close the place down. This historic structure was in use as a warehouse in the 1950s but was then restored as part of the Independence Mall project in Philadelphia.

against the Quaker policy of not supporting the colonists against the British. Led by several young Quakers, among them Samuel Wetherill, some members of the Society of Friends broke off from the religion to support the patriotic cause. They decided they would rather be read out of the community than not support the Revolution.

The Free Quakers were made up of Quakers disowned by the Society of Friends for supporting the Revolutionary War effort. Some Quakers, like John Claypoole, fought in the war, while others sold military supplies that helped the war effort. People in the Society of Friends were expelled simply for taking a loyalty oath to the new American government, asked of them by the Pennsylvania government.

Even though many Quakers were expelled from their faith, the Free Quaker movement was never very large. The movement never grew much after the Revolutionary War either, but it did gain enough members to build and maintain a meetinghouse. The people who did join probably felt they had nowhere else to go because, like Betsy Ross, they had been read out of their religion. They lived the same lifestyle they had previously, and believed almost all of the same things, but their family and religion no longer accepted them. It was natural that these displaced members of the Society of Friends would eventually come together to practice their common beliefs as the Free Quakers.

In 1783, the very year that the Free Quaker meetinghouse was finally built, the British and the Americans signed the Treaty of Paris, officially ending the Revolutionary War. Life in Philadelphia began to get really active again, as the British were no longer blocking supplies into the city. This was good news for John and Betsy because now they could have access to all sorts of new materials for their upholstery business. Also, with more trade happening, and new confidence after their recent victory over Britain, the American people had a little bit more money to spend on upholstered items than they did during the war. Other businesses also felt the effects of renewed confidence and increased spending in the community. All the people of Philadelphia were feeling more optimistic and prosperous than they had in a long time.

11. Life After the War

The end of the Revolutionary War brought increased business and a larger family to John Claypoole and Betsy Ross. They both decided that it was time to move from their home and shop on 89 Arch Street in Philadelphia to a larger house and shop nearby. The house was one of the many old brick colonial houses built by Betsy's great-grandfather, Andrew Griscom. An advertisement in a local paper told of the move of Betsy and John's upholstery shop to a larger location:

> *"Claypoole, John, Upholsterer, Respectfully informs the Public in general, and his Friends and Customers in particular, that he had removed from Arch Street to the Southwest corner of Race and Second Streets, where he continues to carry on the business of Upholsterer In all its various branches, and on as reasonable terms as are possible to live by."*

The year of the move was a busy one for Betsy Ross and her family. In 1786, her eldest daughter by

Joseph Ashburn, Zillah, suddenly died. While Betsy Ross was probably sad, there was little time for grieving as there were many other children running around the new house. In addition to all of this, Betsy and John had just signed up their biggest client, the state government at the Pennsylvania State House. The upholstery shop would make coverings for chairs and desks as well as venetian blinds for the windows. In addition, John also may have made furniture for the state government. This important contract meant that Betsy and John would be putting long hours into the business.

While the couple had their hands full after the war, so did Philadelphia. It had always been a center of political activity in the colonies, but in 1787 it hosted the conference that was to draw up the Constitution of the United States. Back in 1782, while the war raged on, representatives from the colonies had drawn up the Articles of Confederation. The Articles of Confederation were not working well, however, and many states were arguing over taxes, boundary lines, and money. A new constitution was needed to give more power to one central government so that certain things, such as taxes and money, could be organized on a national level. On September 17, 1787, the Constitution was created and the United States was formed.

After the individual states ratified, or decided to accept, the new Constitution, Philadelphia became the

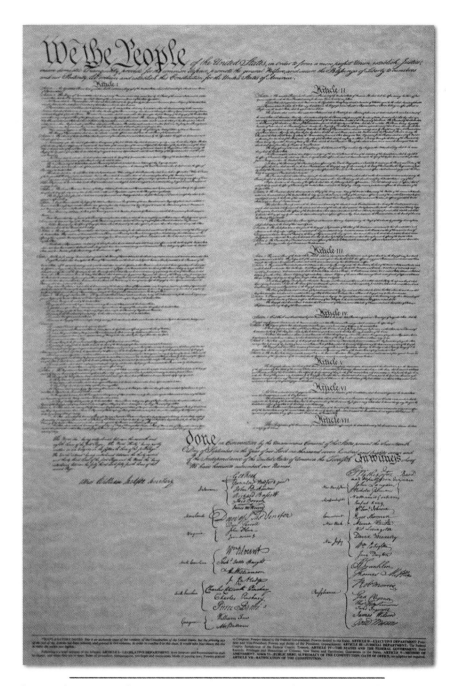

This is the original U.S. Constitution, created in 1787, and approved by the states in 1788. This document and its Bill of Rights have become a model for democratic governments around the world.

national capital in 1790. George Washington, the leader of the Continental army during the Revolutionary War, became the very popular first president. Times in Philadelphia were very exciting, and business for Betsy Ross and John Claypoole continued to be good because of their closeness to the new government, and all of the people involved in it.

After some time working with Betsy in the upholstery shop, John Claypoole got a job working for the new U.S. government at the Philadelphia Customs House. This left Betsy to take care of the upholstery business by herself, a job to which she was accustomed. In 1795, the flag design was changed when Vermont

The White House in Washington, D.C., took a long time to complete. Construction began in October 1792, while George Washington was president. Washington oversaw construction of the house, but he never lived in it. It was not until 1800 that the capital finally moved to the city of Washington. By then, John Adams had become president.

and Kentucky were admitted to the Union. This brought new business to Betsy's shop as orders were placed for the new flag with fifteen stars.

In 1800, Philadelphia finally quieted down somewhat when the capital of the United States was moved to Washington, D.C. Life was still busy for Betsy and her growing family, though, and they soon had to move to an even larger house in Philadelphia.

Betsy Ross had lost two husbands to the Revolutionary War. Her third husband, John Claypoole, had survived the winter in Valley Forge, Pennsylvania, and Old Mill prison in England. These experiences took their toll on his health, and John Claypoole was often ill. John soon could no longer work at the customshouse and was confined to home with his illness.

Betsy Ross again was responsible for making all the money for her family. In June 1812, war again broke out against Great Britain. During the War of 1812, from 1812 to 1814, Betsy made a decent living selling flags to military organizations and shipping firms. Then, after several years of illness, John Claypoole died in August 1817.

Betsy Ross was now a widow for the third time in her life. After her long and happy thirty-four-year marriage to John Claypoole, Betsy would not marry again. Betsy Ross decided to keep her upholstery shop open, and ran it for another ten years after the death of her husband.

Finally, in 1827, Betsy Ross retired. She was seventy-five years old. She turned the ownership and operation of the shop over to her daughter Clarissa and niece, Margaret Boggs. Betsy Ross moved from her house in Philadelphia and lived with her daughters.

In 1834, Betsy Ross and John Wetherill decided to close the Free Quaker meetinghouse. John Wetherill was the grandson of one of the Free Quaker founders, Samuel Wetherill. After the Revolutionary War, the number of Free Quakers had dropped steadily as members passed away, or joined other religions. Betsy Ross continued to go to the Free Quaker meetinghouse faithfully until the day it closed.

After the closing of the Free Quaker meetinghouse, Betsy Ross's health started to decline. She was living

This is Betsy Griscom Ross Ashburn Claypoole's grave at the Betsy Ross House. She was originally buried in Philadelphia's Mount Moriah, about 10 miles (16 km) north of the house. The decision was made to move her grave here after the house was restored. She is buried with her third husband, John Claypoole.

with her daughter Jane and son-in-law Caleb Canby at the time. As her illness got worse, Betsy had to stay in bed. On January 30, 1836, Betsy Griscom Ross Ashburn Claypoole died at the age of 84. Betsy Ross lived longer than most women of her time, and she was witness to the birth of the United States. She was also an active participant in making it happen, as were all of the colonists willing to sacrifice everything for a chance at liberty. Betsy Ross has been buried in three different locations: the Christ Church, Mount Moriah cemetery, and finally in the courtyard adjacent to the restored Betsy Ross House.

Betsy Ross lived a long life. She faced many challenges and did things most women of her time did not, all in addition to her possible role in making the first American flag. Betsy Ross was independent-minded and followed her heart even when it meant being shunned by her family and the Quaker religion for marrying John Ross. She was widowed three times; two of these husbands died in the Revolutionary War. Betsy Ross even owned and operated an upholstery business of her own before, during, and after the fight for independence at a time when women rarely owned businesses. Whether or not Betsy Ross made the first American flag, her life story is an inspirational one of independence and courage.

12. The Legend of Betsy Ross?

When the name Betsy Ross is mentioned, the first thing that pops into most people's minds is the American flag. People do not think of her life or her diverse accomplishments. Countless American school-children over the years have learned that in 1776, Betsy Ross made the first American flag. When some historians began to look for evidence confirming this fact, however, they could not find any. Below is the story of how most people came to believe that Betsy Ross made the first American flag, and why some people do not think that she did.

Betsy Ross told the story of the important and historic meeting she had with George Washington, Robert Morris, and George Ross to her children and grandchildren many times. She told them about how difficult times were in Philadelphia during the

Right: At top is a replica of the famous flag that Betsy Ross is believed to have designed, with thirteen, five-pointed stars representing the thirteen original states. Below is the flag that flies in the United States today. It has fifty stars to represent the fifty states that are currently part of the Union.

This is a picture of the Patterson Mansion, home of the
Pennsylvania Historical Society in 1870, as it appeared in 1904.
Here William Canby would go before the members of the society
to tell his grandmother's story and to present sworn affidavits
from people who had heard Betsy Ross's story firsthand.

Revolution and the occupation by the British army.
In 1870, Betsy Ross's grandson William Canby told
his grandmother's stories to the Pennsylvania
Historical Society.

In his speech and article on the subject, Canby relied
on what he remembered, but he also gathered three
sworn affidavits, or written testimony, from his relatives. These affidavits confirm, from different sources,
that the relatives remember Betsy Ross told them of
her meeting with the three committee members,

Soon after William Canby gave his speech to the Pennsylvania Historical Society, his article about Betsy Ross as the maker of the first flag appeared in *The Harper's New Monthly Magazine*. It would soon appear in textbooks around the country.

George Washington, George Ross, and Robert Morris. Betsy's relatives all talk of this experience and her role in the making of the first American flag.

The result of Canby's speech was a renewed interest in Betsy Ross and the American flag. Some of it was driven by the desire to create more high-profile women heroes of the Revolution. Although many women were very patriotic and supported the war effort through remarkable deeds, it was the Founding Fathers who received all of the attention. Soon after Canby addressed the Pennsylvania Historical Society, the story of Betsy Ross was introduced in textbooks and children began to learn about the role of Betsy Ross in the Revolutionary War.

Amazingly enough, these stories that Betsy Ross told are among the only evidence that exists to prove she actually sewed the first American flag. Historians like to be sure that stories are true before they accept them as fact instead of a myth or a legend. Historians have failed to find other evidence that absolutely proves Betsy Ross was the maker of the flag as she claimed.

They have looked for a reference to the flag committee in records of the Continental Congress, or a reference to the making of the first flag in the diaries or papers of Washington, Ross, or Morris. Historians have also looked at old newspapers, diaries of soldiers, and other records trying to find a receipt for the flag or some other evidence. To date, though, no historians have

Did Francis Hopkinson make the first American flag? Francis Hopkinson was a popular politician, a lawyer, a congressman from New Jersey, and a signer of the Declaration of Independence. He was also a poet and a songwriter. In 1780, he claimed to have designed the first flag of the United States. A year later, Hopkinson gave Congress a bill for his work in creating the first flag, but it was rejected. Hopkinson tried several times to get paid, but he was not successful and finally gave up. Many people billed Congress for services they performed, but Congress often paid them very little if at all. Some people believe that even if Hopkinson designed the first flag of America, Betsy Ross still could have modified the design and sewn it.

found anything besides the word of Betsy Ross that says she made the first American flag.

It is important to note that historians have not been able to find proof that Betsy Ross did not sew the first flag, either. In other words, there is no evidence that someone else sewed the first flag rather than Betsy Ross. So, in the end we are still left with this: Some people believe that Betsy Ross sewed the first American flag, and others believe she did not. It is up to you to study, read the facts, and decide for yourself which theory you believe. Many people have decided that Betsy Ross did not have much reason to make up the story about sewing the first flag.

From reading about Betsy Ross's life, we know that she had a Quaker background and was honest and independent. She believed in the patriot cause and was proud of the new nation that was forming. As an upholsterer with connections to some of the Revolutionary leaders, Betsy Ross would have made a likely choice for a job like sewing a flag for the new nation. Whatever you decide, there is certainly no question that Betsy Ross was a patriot who witnessed and took part in one of the most exciting periods of American history.

Appendix

Affidavit of Sophia B. Hildebrant, Daughter of Clarissa S. Wilson and Granddaughter of Elizabeth Claypoole (Betsy Ross), Affidavit dated May 27, 1870:

I remember to have heard my grandmother Elizabeth Claypoole frequently narrate the circumstance of her having made the first Star Spangled Banner; that it was a specimen flag made to the order of the committee of Congress, acting in conjunction with General Washington, who called upon her personally at her store in Arch Street, below Third Street, Philadelphia, shortly before the Declaration of Independence; that she said that General Washington made a redrawing of the design with his own hands after some suggestions made by her; and that this specimen flag was exhibited in Congress by the committee, with a report, and the flag and report were approved and adopted by the Congress; and she received an unlimited order from

*the committee to make flags for the govern-
ment, and to my knowledge she continued to
manufacture the government flags for about
fifty years, when my mother succeeded her in
the business, in which I assisted. I believe the
facts stated in the foregoing article, entitled
"The First American Flag, and Who Made It,"
are all strictly true.*

*Witness my hand at Philadelphia the
Twenty-seventh day of May* A.D. *1870.*

*Witnesses present: Isaac R. Oakford,
Charles H. Evans, S. B. Hildebrandt.*

●　　●　　●　　●　　●　　●

Affidavit of Margaret Donaldson Boggs, Daughter of Sarah Donaldson, who was a Sister of Elizabeth Claypoole (Betsy Ross), Affidavit dated June 3, 1870:

> *I, Margaret Boggs, of the City of Philadelphia, Widow, do hereby certify that I have heard my aunt, Elizabeth Claypoole say many times, that she made the first Star Spangled Banner that ever was made with her own hands; that she made it on the order of General Washington and a committee of the Continental Congress, who together called personally upon her at her house on the North side Arch Street below Third Street, Philadelphia, some time previously to the Declaration of Independence. That they brought with them a drawing, roughly made, of the proposed flag; that she said it was wrong, and proposed alterations, which Washington and the Committee approved; that one of these alterations was in regard to the number of points of the star; that she said it should be five-pointed, and showed them how to fold a piece of paper in the proper manner, and with one cut of the scissors, to make a five-pointed star; that General Washington sat at a table in her back parlor, where they were, and made a drawing of the flag embodying her suggestions, and that she made the flag*

according to this drawing, and the committee carried it before Congress, by whom it was approved and adopted. That she then received orders to make flags for the government as fast as possible; and from that time forward, for upwards of fifty years she made all the flags made for the United States in Philadelphia, and largely for the other naval stations. I was for many years a member of her family, and aided her in the business. I believe the facts stated in the foregoing article entitled "The First American Flag and Who Made It," which has now been read to me are all strictly true.

Witness my hand at Germantown in the City of Philadelphia, this Third day of June A.D. 1870.

Witnesses present: Charles B. Engle, Stephen T. Beale, Margaret Boggs.

● ● ● ● ● ●

Affidavit of Rachel Fletcher, a daughter of Elizabeth Claypoole (Betsy Ross), Affidavit dated July 31, 1871:

I remember having heard my mother Elizabeth Claypoole say frequently that she, with her own hands, (while she was the widow of John Ross,) made the first Star-spangled Banner that ever was made. I remember to have heard her also say that it was made on the order of a Committee, of whom Col. Ross was one, and that Robert Morris was also one of the Committee. That General Washington, acting in conference with the committee, called with them at her house. This house was on the North side of Arch Street a few doors below Third Street, above Bread Street, a two story house, with attic and a dormer window, now standing, the only one of the row left, the old number being 89; it was formerly occupied by Daniel Niles, Shoemaker. Mother at first lived in the house next East, and when the war came, she moved into the house of Daniel Niles. That it was in the month of June 1776, or shortly before the Declaration of Independence that the committee called on her. That the member of the committee named Ross was an uncle of her deceased husband. That she was previously well acquainted with Washington, and that he had often been in her house in friendly visits, as well as on business. That she had embroidered ruffles for his shirt bosoms and cuffs, and that it was partly owing to his friendship for her that she was chosen to make the flag. That when the committee (with General Washington), came into her store she showed them into her parlor, back of her store; and one of them asked her if she could make a flag and that she replied that she did not know but she could try. That they then showed her a drawing roughly executed, of the flag as it was proposed to be made by the committee, and that she saw in it some defects in its proportions and the arrangement and shape of the stars. That she said it was square and a flag should be one third longer than its width, that the stars were scattered promiscuously over the field, and she said they should be either in lines or in some adopted form as a circle, or a star, and that the stars were six-pointed in the drawing, and she said they should be five-pointed. That the gentlemen of the committee and General Washington very respectfully considered the suggestions and acted upon them, General Washington seating himself at a table with a pencil and paper, altered the drawing and then made a new one according to the suggestions of my mother. That General Washington seemed to her to be the active one in making the design, the others having little or nothing to do with it. That the committee then requested her to call on one of their number, a shipping merchant on the wharf, and then adjourned. That she was punctual to her appointment, and then the gentlemen drew out of a chest an old ship's color which he loaned her to show her how the sewing was done; and also gave her the drawing finished according to her suggestions. That this drawing was done in water colors by William Barrett, an artist, who lived on the North side of Cherry Street above Third Street, a large three story brick house on the West side of an alley which ran back to the "Pennsylvania Academy for Young Ladies," kept by James A. Neal, the best school of the kind in the city at that time. That Barrett only did the painting, and had nothing to do with the design. He was often employed by mother afterwards to paint the coats of arms of the United States and of the States on silk flags. That other designs had also been made by the committee and given to other seamstresses to make, but that they were not approved. That mother went diligently to work upon her flag and soon finished it, and returned it, the first star-spangled banner that ever was made, to her employers, that it was run up to the peak of one of the vessels belong-

ing to one of the committee then lying at the wharf, and was received with shouts of applause by the few bystanders who happened to be looking on. That the committee on the same day carried the flag into the Congress sitting in the State House, and made a report presenting the flag and the drawing and that Congress unanimously approved and accepted the report. That the next day Col. Ross called upon my mother and informed her that her work had been approved and her flag adopted, and he gave orders for the purchase of all the materials and the manufacture of as many flags as she could make. And that from that time forward, for over fifty years she continued to make flags for the United States Government.

I believe the facts stated in the foregoing Article entitled "The First American Flag and Who Made It," are all strictly true. This affidavit having been signed by Rachel Fletcher with violet ink, the signature has faded, but is at this time, Seventh Month 24th, 1908, still plainly legible.

Rachel Fletcher

I, Mary Fletcher Wigert, daughter of the said Rachel Fletcher, recognize the signature in the rectangular space outlined in black above, as the signature of my mother Rachel Fletcher.

Mary Fletcher Wigert

Signed in the presence of Mary W. Miller Philadelphia Seventh Mo. 24th, 1908

State of New York

City of New York SS

On the 31st day of July A.D. 1871. Before me the subscriber a Notary Public in and for the Commonwealth of New York, duly commissioned, residing in the said City of New York, personally appeared the above named Rachel Fletcher, who being duly affirmed did depose and say that the statements above certified to by her are all strictly true according to the best of her knowledge and belief, and that she is a daughter of Elizabeth Claypoole. Affirmed and subscribed before me the day and year aforesaid. Witness my hand and Notarial Seal.

Th. J. McEvily

Notary Public City & Co. New York

Timeline

1752   Betsy Ross is born Elizabeth Griscom in West Jersey, Pennsylvania.

1754   The Griscom family moves to Philadelphia.

French and Indian War begins.

1764   Betsy Ross finishes school.

Griscom family moves to the house on Arch Street in Philadelphia.

Apprenticeship for Betsy Ross begins at John Webster's upholstery shop.

1765   The Stamp Act is passed by British parliament.

1768   A British force sails into Boston on September 30.

1770   The Boston Massacre occurs on March 5.

1773   Betsy and John Ross are married.

Betsy and John Ross open an upholstery shop in Philadelphia.

The Boston Tea Party occurs on December 16.

1774 Betsy Ross is read out of the Quaker community.

General Gage and the British government close Boston Harbor.

The First Continental Congress meets in Philadelphia.

1775 The Battle of Lexington and Concord occurs on April 19.

The Second Continental Congress meets in Philadelphia.

The Continental army is formed under the command of George Washington.

1776 John Ross dies on January 21.

British troops leave Boston in March.

Betsy Ross is said to have made the first American flag.

The Declaration of Independence is signed.

1777	Congress adopts the flag made by Betsy Ross as the American flag.
	Betsy Ross marries Joseph Ashburn.
	The British occupy Philadelphia.
1778	The British leave Philadelphia.
1779	Betsy Ross has her first child with John Ashburn.
1780	The Free Quakers begin meeting informally.
1781	The British army surrenders.
1782	John Ashburn dies in a British prison.
1783	The Treaty of Paris is signed, ending the Revolutionary War. America gains her independence from Britain.
	Betsy Ross marries John Claypoole.
1787	The U.S. Constitution is signed.
1795	Kentucky and Vermont are admitted into the Union, and the design of the flag is changed.
1812	The War of 1812 begins between the United States and Great Britain.

1817 John Claypoole dies.

1827 Betsy Ross retires and lives with her daughters.

1834 The Free Quakers close their meeting-house.

1836 Betsy Ross dies on January 30.

1870 William Canby, grandson of Betsy Ross, makes public the stories of his grand-mother's role in making the first American flag.

Glossary

ammunition (am-yoo-NIH-shun) Bullets and gunpowder used in firing a gun or cannon.

apprentice (uh-PREN-tis) A person learning a trade or an art from a skilled worker.

artillery (ar-TIH-luhr-ee) Cannons, or other weapons for firing missiles such as cannonballs.

artisan (AR-tih-zen) An older term for a mechanic or craftsman. A person with a certain type of job, usually involving manual labor, and the production or repair of material items. Silversmiths, carpenters, shipbuilders, blacksmiths, and tailors would have been considered artisans.

broadsides (BRAHD-sydz) Large sheets or pages, often printed on both sides, that had current news of the day or advertisements, like a short newspaper.

canton (KAN-ton) The top inner corner of a flag.

depression (di-PREH-shun) A period of low economic activity, slow growth, and high unemployment, or fewer jobs.

duties (DOO-teez) Taxes or fees on goods.

eloped (i-LOHPT) To have obtained a marriage without a formal ceremony, often done quickly and against the wishes of parents.

emigrated (EH-mih-grayt-id) To have left a country of which one is a native to go to another country to live permanently.

express rider (ik-SPRES RY-derz) A person who spreads news, alarms, and warnings between towns and cities in the colonies, usually on horseback.

loyalist (LOY-uh-list) A colonist who was loyal to the British government and wanted to remain under the rule of Britain. Also called a Tory.

militia (muh-LIH-shuh) A part-time army made up of citizens who come together and train and fight on behalf of their town or county.

minutemen (MIH-net-men) A specialized group of soldiers within a militia who were trained to be ready for battle at a moment's notice.

modified (MAH-duh-fyd) Changed or altered in some way.

muster (MUHS-ter) The act of coming together, especially as a military group.

Parliament (PAR-lih-mint) The lawmaking, or

legislative, body in Britain that is similar to Congress in the United States.

privateer (pry-vuh-TEER) A captain who runs a private ship that profits from the merchant trade during war but is not part of the Navy.

prosperity (prah-SPEHR-ih-tee) Good economic times, usually when many people have jobs and more money.

ratify (RA-tih-fy) To approve by popular vote.

sampler (SAM-pler) A picture that is made by sewing, or embroidering with a needle and thread.

smuggling (SMUH-gling) To carry cargo into or out of a country against the laws or without paying the taxes of that country.

stockpiling (STAHK-pyl-ing) Gathering large amounts.

Tory (TOHR-ee) A colonist who was loyal to the British government and wanted to remain under the rule of Britain. More commonly he or she was called a loyalist.

Whig (WIG) A colonist who believed the British were treating the colonies unfairly and wanted independence from Britain. These people were often called patriots.

Additional Resources

To learn more about Betsy Ross, the American Revolution, and life in colonial America, check out these books and Web sites.

Books

Miller, Susan Martins, and Arthur M. Schlesinger, ed. *Betsy Ross: American Patriot*. New York: Chelsea House Publishers, 2000.

St. George, Judith. *Betsy Ross: Patriot of Philadelphia*. New York: Henry Holt and Company, 1997.

Weil, Ann. *Betsy Ross, Designer of Our Flag*. New York: Aladdin Books, 1983.

Web Sites

www.fortmifflin.org/

www.icss.com/usflag/about.betsy.ross.html

www.ushistory.org/betsy/index.html

Bibliography

Betsy Ross House Archives. *Pennsylvania Gazette, articles 1766-83, files, notebooks, etc.* Philadelphia.

Boorstein, Daniel J. *The Americans: The Colonial Experience.* New York: Random House, 1958.

Elgin, Kathleen. *The Quakers: The Religious Society of Friends.* New York: David McKay, 1968.

Miller, Susan Martins, and Arthur M. Schlesinger, ed. *Betsy Ross: American Patriot.* New York: Chelsea House Publishers, 2000.

St. George, Judith. *Betsy Ross: Patriot of Philadelphia.* New York: Henry Holt and Company, 1997.

Index

About the Author

Ryan P. Randolph is a writer with an avid interest in history. Ryan has a Bachelor of Arts degree in both history and political science from Colgate University in Hamilton, New York. Ryan is also a member of the history honor society Phi Alpha Theta. He works in a financial consulting firm and lives with his wife in New York City.

Credits

Photo Credits

P. 4 Courtesy Charles H. Weisgerber II?; p. 6 © George Lepp/ CORBIS; pp. 10, 33, 50, 66 © Bettmann/CORBIS; pp. 11, 12, 20-21, 23, 31, 37, 42 (top), 52, 67, 89 © CORBIS; pp. 14, 60 © North Wind Pictures; p. 17 Rare Book Department, The Free Library of Philadelphia; p. 18 Philadelphia Museum of Art: Gift of Sally Wistar Ingersoll Fox; p. 26 Friends Historical Library, Swarthmore College; pp. 27, 82 © Maura Boruchow, courtesy Besty Ross House; p. 28 Gloucester County Historical Society, Woodbury, NJ; pp. 29, 74 © Lee Snider/CORBIS; p. 36 © Arthur D'Arazien/SuperStock; pp. 38, 44, 55, 85 (top) Courtesy of The Rosen Publishing Group, Inc.; pp. 41, 57 © Archive Photos; pp. 42 (bottom), 70 © Hulton Getty/Archive Photos; pp. 46-47, 63 © SuperStock; p. 53 Pennsylvania State Archives, Records of the Pennsylvania's Revolutionary Governments, (RG 27), Minutes of the Navy Board; p. 54 Papers of the Continental Congress, Records of the Continental and Confederation Congresses and the Constitutional Convention, Record Group 360; p. 56 © Stock Montage/SuperStock; p. 62 © The Granger Collection, New York; p. 64 Courtesy of the Map Division, The New York Public Library, Astor, Lenox and Tilden Foundations; p. 71 Courtesy Gerald Prior/Central Library, Plymouth; p. 73 Courtesy the American Philosophical Society, Records of the Society of Free Quakers; p. 79 © Joseph Sohm, Visions of America/CORBIS; p. 80 © CORBIS-BETTMANN; p. 85 (bottom) © Joseph Sohm; ChromoSohm, Inc./CORBIS; p. 86 Courtesy of the Historical of Pennsylvania Society, (Society Collection); p. 87 The Harper's New Monthly Magazine.

Series Design
Laura Murawski

Layout Design
Corinne Jacob

Project Editor
Joanne Randolph

Photo Researcher
Jeffrey Wendt